learn to draw
Polar Animals

Draw more than 25 favorite Arctic & Antarctic wildlife critters

ILLUSTRATED BY ROBBIN CUDDY

Publisher: Rebecca J. Razo
Creative Director: Shelley Baugh
Project Editor: Elizabeth Gilbert
Senior Editor: Stephanie Meissner
Managing Editor: Karen Julian
Associate Editor: Jennifer Gaudet
Assistant Editor: Janessa Osle
Production Designers: Debbie Aiken, Amanda Tannen
Production Manager: Nicole Szawlowski
Production Coordinator: Lawrence Marquez

www.walterfosterjr.com
3 Wrigley, Suite A
Irvine, CA 92618

1 3 5 7 9 10 8 6 4 2

Table of Contents

Tools & Materials 4

How to Use This Book 5

Adélie Penguin 6

Woolly Bear Caterpillar 8

Tundra Swan 10

Arctic Hare 12

Arctic Tern 14

Red Fox 16

Beluga Whale 18

Dall Sheep 20

Canada Lynx 22

Caribou 24

Blue Whale 26

Elephant Seal 28

Emperor Penguin 30

Ermine 32

Humpback Whale 34

Harp Seal 36

Killer Whale 38

Polar Bear 40

Macaroni Penguin 42

Musk-Ox 44

Narwhal 46

Leopard Seal 48

Puffin 50

Arctic Wolf 52

Sled Dog 54

Arctic Fox 56

Snowy Owl 58

Albatross 60

Walrus 62

Mini Quiz Answers 64

Tools & Materials

There's more than one way to bring polar animals to life on paper—
you can use crayons, markers, colored pencils, or even paints.
Just be sure you have plenty of good "polar colors"—
blues, purples, grays, and browns.

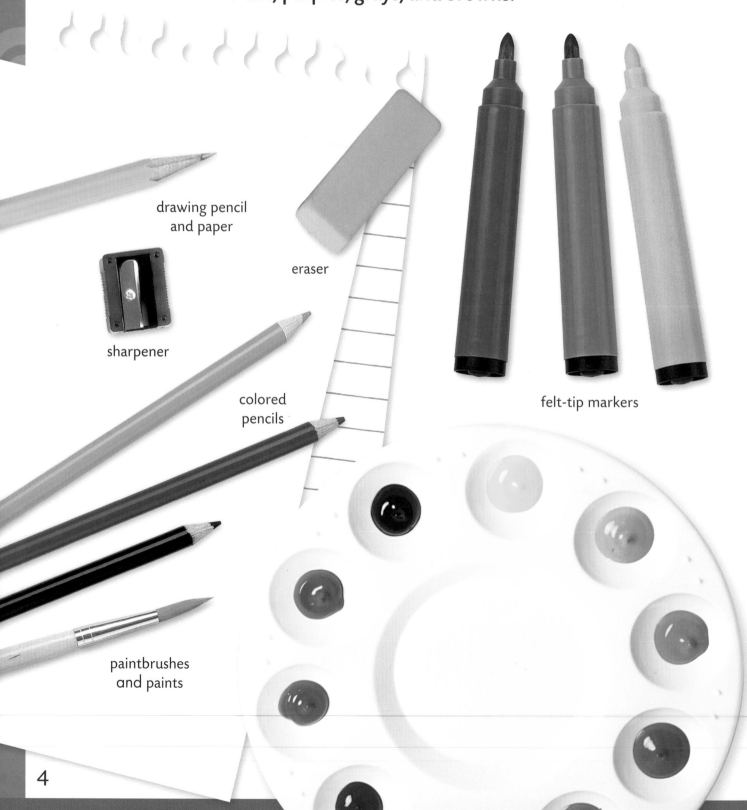

drawing pencil
and paper

eraser

sharpener

colored
pencils

felt-tip markers

paintbrushes
and paints

How to Use This Book

The drawings in this book are made up of basic shapes, such as circles, triangles, and rectangles. Practice drawing the shapes below.

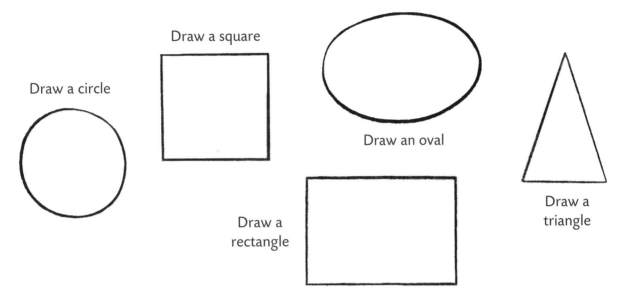

Draw a square

Draw a circle

Draw an oval

Draw a rectangle

Draw a triangle

Notice how these drawings begin with basic shapes.

In this book, you'll learn about the size, location, diet, and appearance of each featured polar animal. Look for mini quizzes along the way to learn new and interesting facts!

Look for this symbol, and check your answers on page 64!

Adélie Penguin

Size: 27-1/2 inches in length
Weight: 13 lbs

Location: Coasts and ice shelves of Antarctica

Diet: Krill, fish, and squid

Did You Know?

Penguins aren't born with their trademark black-and-white feather pattern. Newborn chicks are often black or light gray!

These adorable birds have a small ring of white feathers around each eye. They also have longer feathers along the tops of their heads that can form small crests.

Mini Quiz

How long do Adélie penguins live?

(Answer on page 64)

Woolly Bear Caterpillar

Size: 1-1/2 to 2 inches in length
Location: Canadian Arctic
Diet: Herbs, forbs, grasses, and tree leaves

Did You Know?

It is believed that measuring a woolly bear caterpillar's segments can predict the weather! Thicker-than-usual black bands point to upcoming severe winter conditions.

Woolly bear caterpillars are bristly critters with a brownish-orange band down the center and a black band at each end. They eventually hatch into tiger moths.

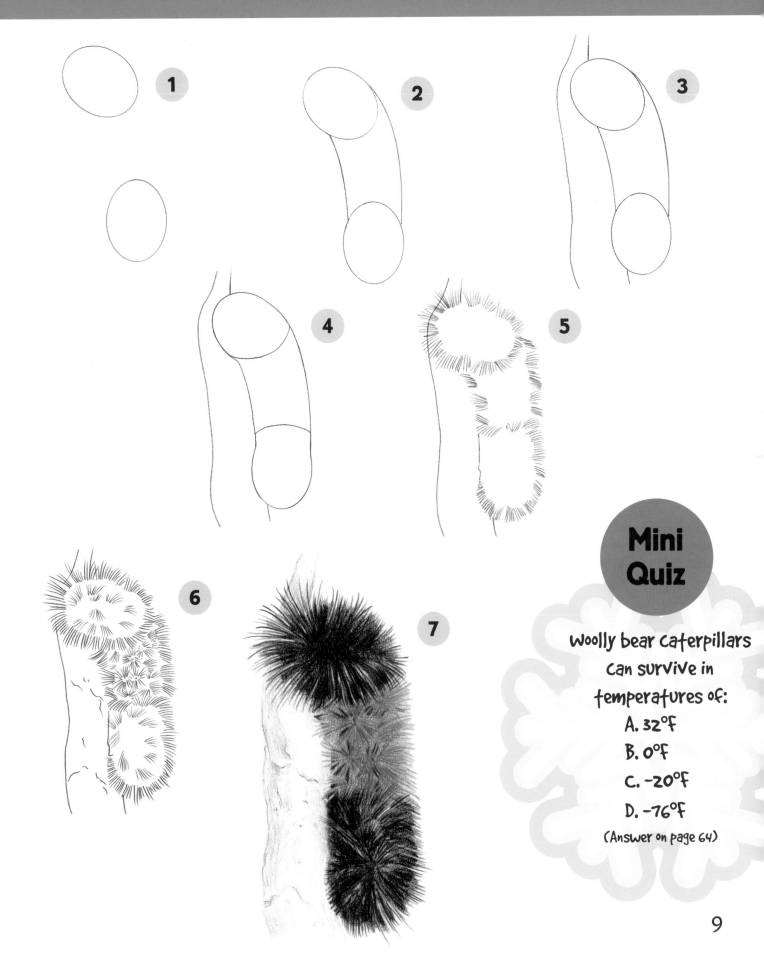

1

2

3

4

5

6

7

Mini Quiz

Woolly bear caterpillars can survive in temperatures of:

A. 32°F

B. 0°F

C. -20°F

D. -76°F

(Answer on page 64)

Tundra Swan

Details

Size: 50 inches in length
Weight: 16 lbs
Location: Canada and Alaska, migrating to Southern California and North Carolina for winter
Diet: Aquatic plants, reeds, grasses, and herbs

Did You Know?

The tundra swan holds its neck horizontally as it flies and vertically as it swims.

This elegant, white-feathered bird has a long, curving neck and a black bill, feet, and legs.

1

2

3

4

5

6

7

Fun Fact!

Tundra swans' wings produce a whistling sound while in flight, earning them the name "whistling swans."

11

Arctic Hare

Location: North American tundra

Size: 20–25 inches in length
Weight: 6–15 lbs

Did You Know?

During non-snowy months, the Arctic hare's coat develops some gray to blend in with its rocky surroundings.

Diet: Mosses, lichens, woody plants, berries, and leaves

This hare has a beautiful coat of thick, white fur. Its ears are tipped with black and are shorter than the ears of most hares.

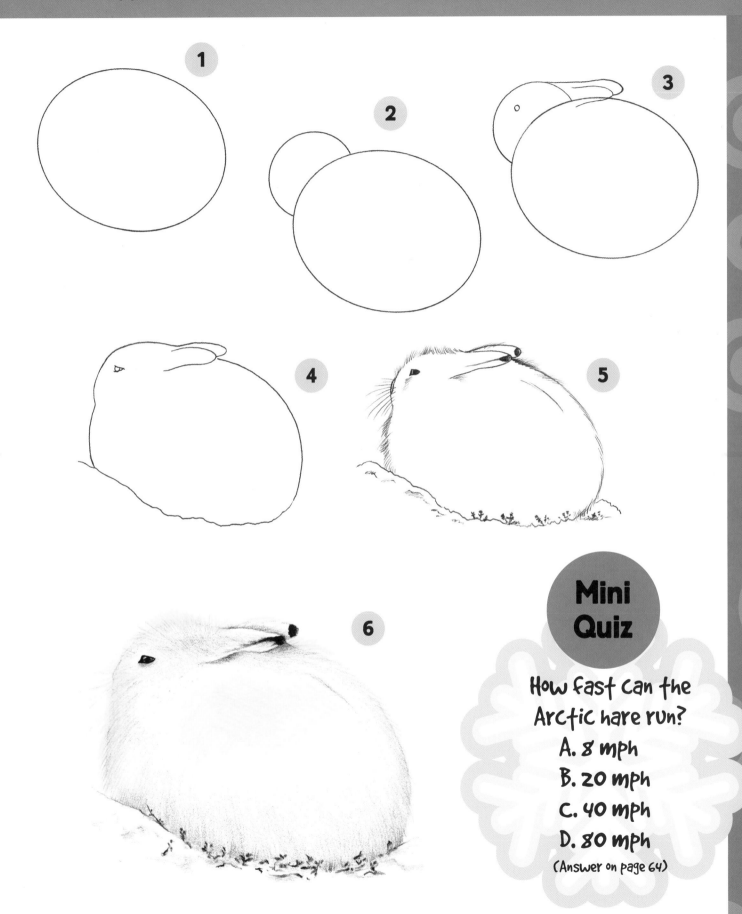

1

2

3

4

5

6

Mini Quiz

How fast can the Arctic hare run?
A. 8 mph
B. 20 mph
C. 40 mph
D. 80 mph
(Answer on page 64)

Arctic Tern

Location: Southern Arctic regions to Antarctica

Fun Fact! This bird is known for traveling long distances to migrate, and can reach more than 44,000 miles roundtrip!

Diet: Fish, crustaceans, insects, worms, and berries

Size: 15 inches in length
Weight: Up to 2 lbs

The Arctic tern has a rounded head with a black-cap marking.
Its tail has a deep fork, and its beak, legs, and feet are bright red.

Did You Know?

The Arctic tern's gray wings have a span of roughly 33 inches.

Red Fox

Size: 40 inches in length (including tail)
Weight: 10–15 lbs

Location: Arctic tundra to desert regions

Diet: Mice, rabbits, birds, eggs, and fruit

Did You Know?

The red fox can be found on five of the seven continents: Europe, Asia, North America, Africa, and Australia.

The sleek red fox has a reddish-brown coat with black on its legs, tail, and triangular ears. Its fluffy tail often has a white tip.

Fun Fact!

The red fox has cat-like eyes with vertical slits for pupils.

Beluga Whale

Details

Size: 15 feet in length
Weight: 3,000 lbs
Location: Coast of the
Arctic Ocean
Diet: Fish, crab, squid

Did You Know?

Belugas have
34 teeth for
capturing prey:
nine pairs on the
top and eight pairs
on the bottom.

The beluga whale is a beautiful white mammal that lacks a dorsal fin. It has a distinct bulbous forehead, along with a flexible head and neck.

1

2

3

4

5

6

7

Mini Quiz

True or false: The beluga whale is found only in the ocean.

(Answer on page 64)

19

Dall Sheep

Size: 3 feet tall at the shoulders
Weight: 225 lbs

Location: Alaska and Western Canada

Diet: Grasses, plants, and mosses

Did You Know?

Bears, wolves, and coyotes are the main predators of Dall sheep.

These thinhorn sheep have beautiful white coats, yellow eyes, and amber horns. Their hooves have two flexible toes that help them walk on rocky terrain.

Mini Quiz

What are some differences between male and female Dall sheep?

(Answer on page 64)

Canada Lynx

Location: North American forests

Size: 3 feet in length
Weight: 18–30 lbs

Diet: Snowshoe hares, mice, birds, and squirrels

Fun Fact!

The lynx is known for its keen sense of sight and excellent hearing, which make it an effective hunter!

This exotic-looking wildcat has a grayish-brown coat,
a short tail, a facial ruff, and ears tipped with black tufts of hair.

1

2

Mini Quiz

True or false:
The Canada lynx
is active during
the day.
(Answer on page 64)

3

4

5

7

6

23

Caribou

Details

Size: 4 feet tall at the shoulders
Weight: 550 lbs
Location: Arctic tundra and forests of Canada, Alaska, Europe, Asia, and Greenland
Diet: Grasses, plants, mushrooms, and lichens

Fun Fact!

Caribou have large, hollow hooves that help them dig in snow and paddle through water!

Also called "reindeer," caribou are deer with long legs and impressive antlers. A male caribou's antlers can reach 5 feet in length and have up to 40 points!

True or False:
Both male and
female caribou
have antlers.
(Answer on page 64)

Mini Quiz

Blue Whale

Size: 100 feet in length
Weight: 150 tons (300,000 lbs)

Diet:
Krill

Location:
All oceans, primarily near Antarctica

Blue whales are so large that their hearts alone can weigh around 1,500 pounds!

Fun Fact!

This massive ocean dweller is blue-gray in color with areas of light gray. It has a very small dorsal fin and grooves that run along the underside of its body.

Mini Quiz

True or false:
The blue whale is
the largest animal
that has ever lived
on earth.
(Answer on page 64)

Elephant Seal

Size: 21 feet in length
Weight: 4 tons (8,000 lbs)

Diet: Fish and squid

Did You Know?

The elephant seal's color ranges from yellow-brown to blue-gray.

Location: Coasts of California and Baja California; subantarctic regions

This large, loud seal is named for the male's trunk-like snout, which can inflate to produce a "warning" noise for other males.

1

2

3

4

5

6

7

Mini Quiz

What are female elephant seals called? What are male elephant seals called?

(Answer on page 64)

Emperor Penguin

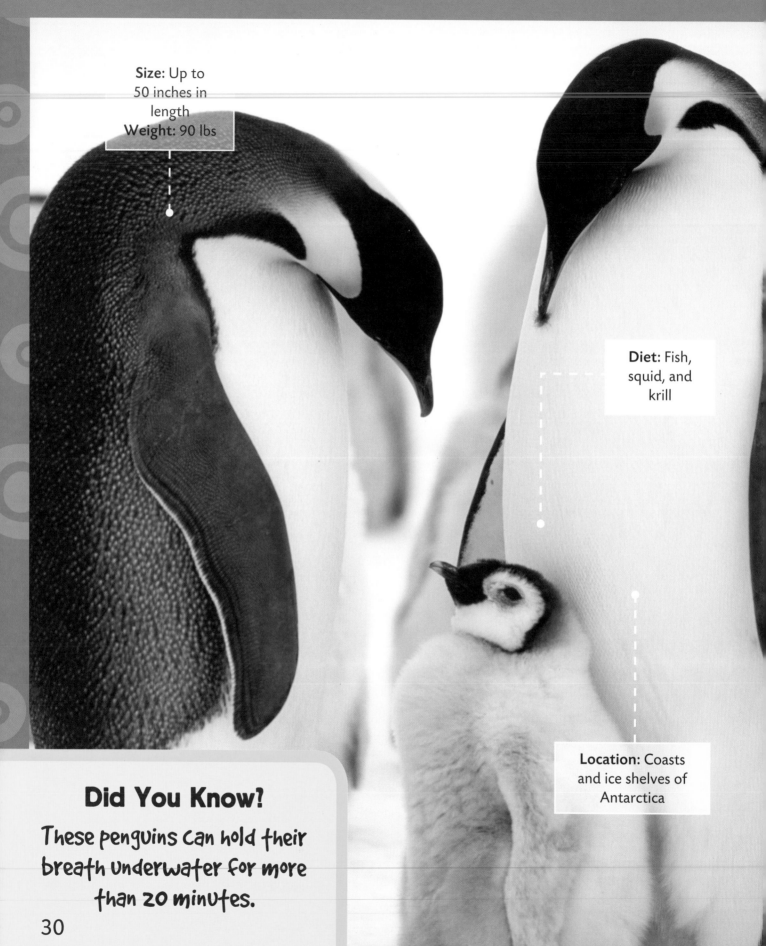

Size: Up to 50 inches in length
Weight: 90 lbs

Diet: Fish, squid, and krill

Location: Coasts and ice shelves of Antarctica

Did You Know?

These penguins can hold their breath underwater for more than 20 minutes.

Emperor penguins have sleek, regal black-and-white coloring, with yellow and orange accents on the neck and chest.

Fun Fact!

The female lays one egg per breeding season, which the male keeps warm by balancing between his feet and body.

31

Ermine

Location:
North America and Eurasia

Size: 13 inches in length (including the tail)
Weight: 7 oz

Diet: Mice, lemmings, squirrels, birds, and fish

Did You Know?

The ermine has several names, including short-tailed weasel, Bonaparte weasel, and stoat.

This adorable weasel has a long body, short legs, and a black-tipped tail. To blend in with the snow, its coat turns from mostly brown to white during the winter.

Mini Quiz

True or false: Male and female ermines are the same size.

(Answer on page 64)

Humpback Whale

Details

Size: 52 feet in length
Weight: 40 tons (80,000 lbs)
Location: All oceans, from the polar regions to the tropics
Diet: Krill, plankton, and fish

Did You Know?

These musical animals communicate with each other using complex "songs." They also use sounds to hunt and navigate.

The humpback whale has large tail flukes and tubercles (whisker-like bumps) around the mouth. It is often seen breaching or leaping from the water!

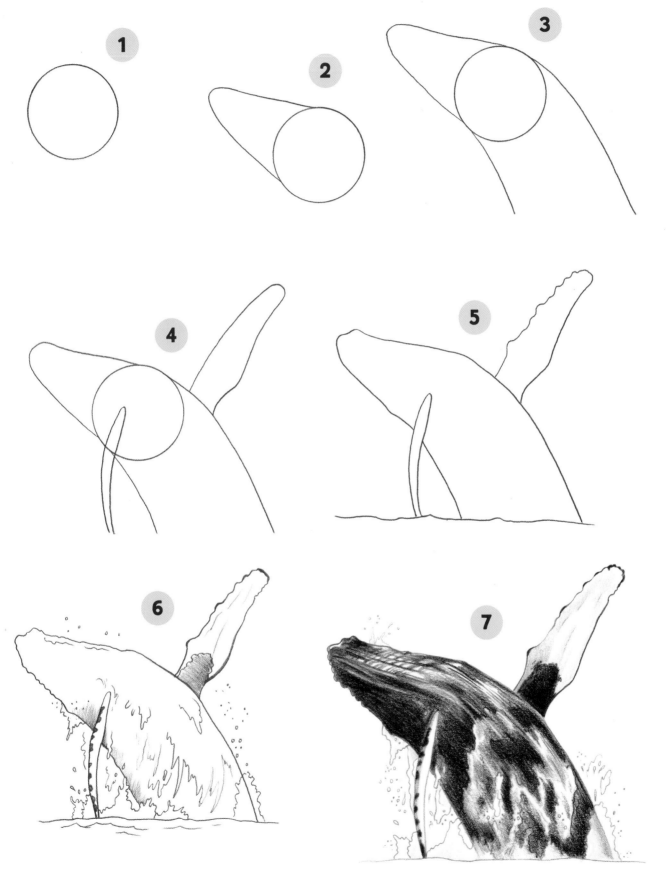

Harp Seal

Details

Size: 6 feet in length
Weight: 300 lbs
Location: North Atlantic and Arctic oceans
Diet: Small fish and crustaceans

Mini Quiz

What is a baby seal called?
A. Calf
B. Kitten
C. Pup
D. Cub

(Answer on page 64)

Adult harp seals are gray with black markings on their backs that resemble harps or saddles.

1

2

3

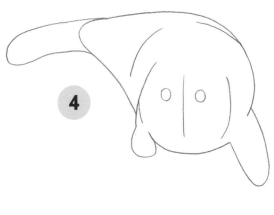

4

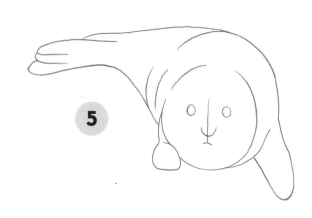

5

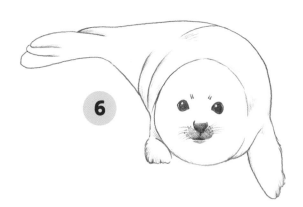

6

7

Killer Whale

Details

Size: 26 feet in length
Weight: 5 tons (10,000 lbs)
Location: Polar regions to the equator
Diet: Seals, sea lions, fish, squid, birds, and sometimes whales

Did You Know?

Orcas are social animals that live and hunt in small groups called "pods." Each pod uses its own set of sounds to communicate.

Also called "orcas," these intelligent and distinctly colored mammals are black with white underbellies and patches.

Fun Fact!

Killer whales are actually large dolphins—not whales!

Polar Bear

Location: Arctic island coastlines and ice shelves

Size: 8 feet in length
Weight: 1,600 lbs

Did You Know?

These powerful, patient hunters have no predators in the wild.

Diet: Seals, small walruses, and sometimes small whales

Polar bears have a thick coat of white fur and long hind legs. They also have large, hairy feet and sharp claws that help them walk safely on ice.

Fun Fact!

Polar bears have black skin under their fur to help them absorb warmth from the sun.

Macaroni Penguin

Size: 20–28 inches in length
Weight: 12 lbs

Location: Rocky coasts and islands of Antarctica, plus islands in the southern Indian and Atlantic oceans

Diet: Krill, crustaceans, squid, and small fish

Did You Know?

There are more Macaroni penguins on earth than any other species of penguin.

This penguin has a distinct yellow-orange crown of feathers on its head. It also has a red bill, red eyes, and a black face.

1

2

3

Fun Fact!

British explorers named the Macaroni penguin because its yellow feathers reminded them of a stylish hat worn in the 18th century, called a "macaroni."

4

5

6

7

Musk-Ox

Details

Size: Up to 5 feet tall at the shoulders
Weight: Up to 800 lbs
Location: North America, Greenland, Siberia, and Scandinavia
Diet: Lichens, mosses, roots, and leafy plants

Did You Know?

In the winter, musk-oxen live and travel in herds of 30 or more, which helps them defend against attacking wolves and dogs.

These cold-weather beasts have long, shaggy brown hair; horns that curve down and out from the face; and hooves that help them walk in the snow.

Fun Fact!

The musk-ox's coat is made up of an outer layer of coarse "guard hairs" and an undercoat of "qiviut" (short, insulating hair). The coat protects them from the cold temperatures of the Arctic.

Narwhal

Details

Size: 17 feet in length
Weight: Up to 3,500 lbs
Location: Arctic coasts and rivers
Diet: Fish, squid, and shrimp

Did You Know?

Only three species of whale live in Arctic waters year-round, including narwhal, beluga, and bowhead whales.

The narwhal is a spotted gray whale with flippers that turn up at the tips. Male narwhals have one long tusk that grows straight out from the upper jaw.

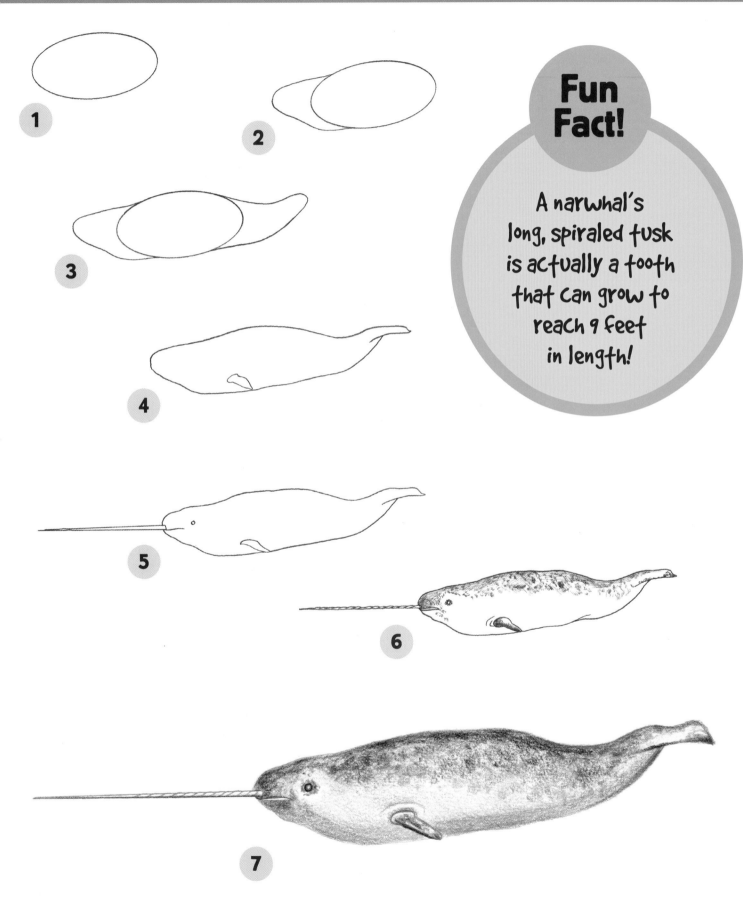

Fun Fact!

A narwhal's long, spiraled tusk is actually a tooth that can grow to reach 9 feet in length!

Leopard Seal

Details

Size: 12 feet in length
Weight: Roughly 850 lbs
Location: Arctic and Antarctic coasts and waters
Diet: Penguins, fish, shellfish, squid, and other seals

Mini Quiz

True or false: Leopard seals are the only seals that eat warm-blooded animals.

(Answer on page 64)

The leopard seal has a large head and a gray coat with black spots. A fierce and loud predator, this seal sports a set of long, triangular teeth.

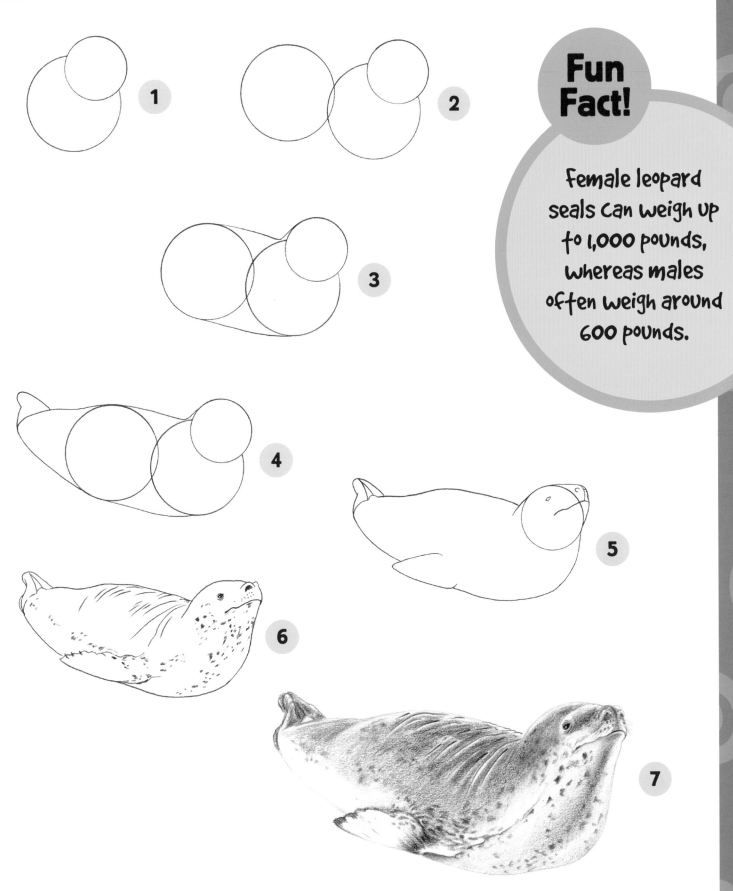

1

2

3

Fun Fact!

Female leopard seals can weigh up to 1,000 pounds, whereas males often weigh around 600 pounds.

4

5

6

7

Puffin

Location: Coasts and oceans of North America, Iceland, and northern Asia

Size: 12 inches in length
Weight: About 1 lb

Diet: Small fish and eels

Fun Fact!

The puffin is known for its distinct beak, which is blue-gray in the winter and bright orange in the spring.

Sometimes called a "sea parrot," this diving bird has a tall, triangular beak and black-and-white markings. Puffins spend the majority of their lives at sea.

Mini Quiz

Where are most of the world's puffins found?

A. Northeastern coast of North America

B. Iceland

C. Northeastern coast of Canada

D. Northern Asia

(Answer on page 64)

1

2

3

4

5

6

7

51

Arctic Wolf

Size: Up to 6 feet in length
Weight: 75–125 lbs

Diet: Large herbivores (such as musk-oxen and caribou), small game, seals, and birds

Location: North America and Greenland

Did You Know?

The Arctic wolf is known for its big, sharp teeth; strong jaws; and impressive endurance. They can consume up to 20 pounds of meat in one meal!

The Arctic wolf has a short muzzle, small ears, and a thick, double-coat of white fur that keeps it dry and warm in subzero Arctic temperatures.

Mini Quiz

What is the term for a group of Arctic wolves that hunt and travel together?
A. Pack
B. Pod
C. Herd
D. Kennel
(Answer on page 64)

53

Sled Dog

Details

Size: Anywhere from 35–150 lbs, most sled dogs weigh about 60 lbs
Location: Northern Europe, North America, and Siberia
Diet: Dry kibble supplemented with meat and animal fat

Mini Quiz

Which of the following breeds is NOT considered a sled dog:
A. Alaskan Malamute
B. Golden Retriever
C. Eskimo Dog
D. Samoyed

(Answer on page 64)

With thick coats to protect them from frigid temperatures, sled dogs are fast, hardy canines that work in teams to pull sleds through snow and over ice.

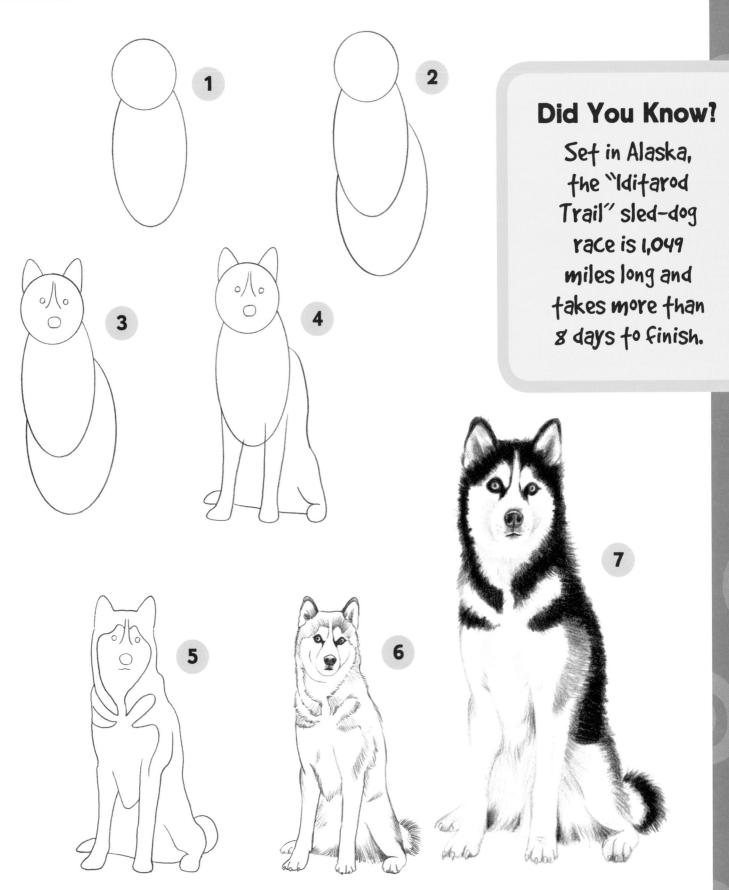

Did You Know?

Set in Alaska, the "Iditarod Trail" sled-dog race is 1,049 miles long and takes more than 8 days to finish.

Arctic Fox

Details

Size: 2 feet in length
Weight: 7–17 lbs
Location: Arctic tundra and seaside mountains
Diet: Small animals and vegetables

Did You Know?

Arctic foxes are scavengers as well as hunters. These cunning canines are known for feeding on scraps left behind by polar bears.

Arctic foxes have beautiful, thick coats of fur and full, bushy tails. Their coats range from blue-gray to brown and white, changing with the seasons.

Fun Fact!

Also known as "polar foxes" or "white foxes," Arctic foxes have fur on the soles of their feet to protect them from the snowy, icy ground of the tundra.

Snowy Owl

Location: Arctic tundra and areas of North America, Asia, and Europe

Size: 2 feet in length
Weight: About 5 lbs

Diet: Lemmings, hares, rodents, birds, and fish

Fun Fact!

Snowy owls build their nests on the ground, right out in the open!

The snowy owl has piercing yellow eyes and white feathers that blend into snow. Males are often white, but youngsters and females have dark markings.

Mini Quiz

True or false: The snowy owl is nocturnal, which means that it is most active at night.
(Answer on page 64)

Albatross

Location:
Northern and
southern oceans

Size: 3–4 feet
in length
Weight: Up
to 22 lbs

Diet: Squid

Fun Fact!

The wandering albatross sports a wingspan of 11 feet! Its lengthy, narrow wings allow it to glide through the air for long periods of time.

The albatross is an enormous seabird with a long wingspan and a long life span. It has a pink beak with a hooked profile and sharp tip.

Did You Know?

Many maritime legends surround the albatross. Sailors commonly believed that killing an albatross would bring bad luck and bad weather to their ship.

Walrus

Details

Size: Up to 12 feet in length
Weight: About 1½ tons (3,000 lbs)
Location: Arctic Ocean
Diet: Shellfish, fish, and sometimes small seals

Did You Know?

The walrus uses its stiff and sensitive whiskers to find food along the ocean floor.

The walrus is a large, blubbery animal with a small head, whiskers, large tusks, and flat front flippers. These social animals often live in large groups.

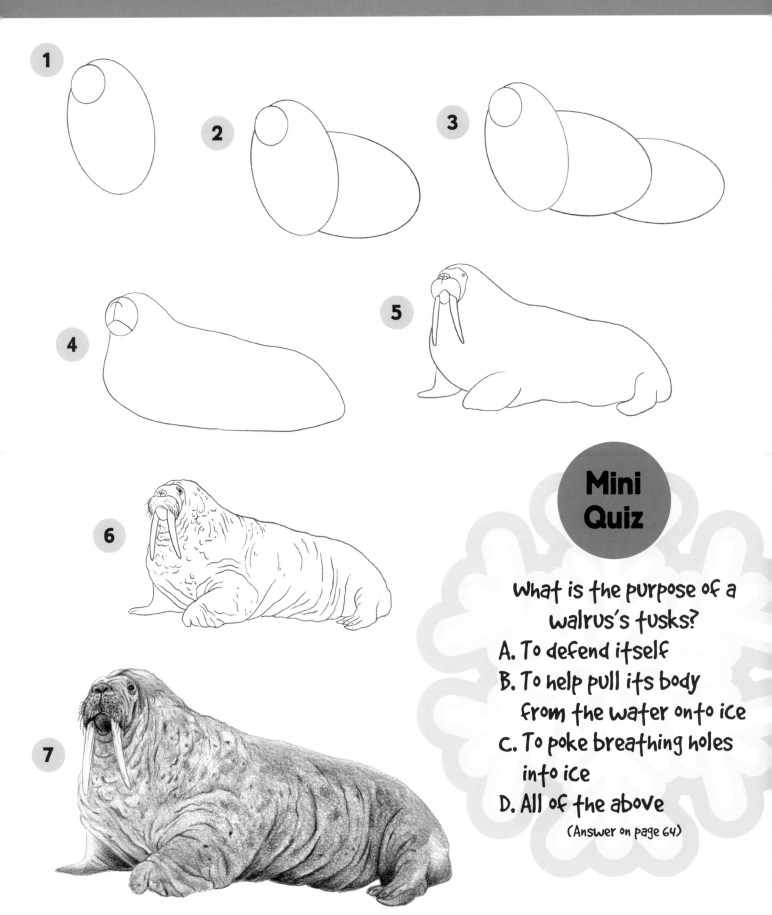

Mini Quiz

What is the purpose of a walrus's tusks?

A. To defend itself
B. To help pull its body from the water onto ice
C. To poke breathing holes into ice
D. All of the above

(Answer on page 64)

Mini Quiz Answers

Page 7: Adélie penguins can live as long as 20 years.

Page 9: D. Woolly bear caterpillars can survive in temperatures below -76°F!

Page 13: C. The swift Arctic hare can run as fast as 40 miles per hour.

Page 19: False. Beluga whales can be found in rivers, as they feed on salmon returning to sea.

Page 21: Female Dall sheep (called "ewes") are smaller than males (called "rams"). Females also have small, slender horns compared to the large, curling horns of the male.

Page 23: False. The Canada lynx is one of the most elusive wild animals. They are active at night and avoid contact with humans, making them a challenge to spot.

Page 25: True. Caribou are the only deer in which females can have antlers too!

Page 27: True. The blue whale is even larger than any dinosaur that ever existed.

Page 29: Female elephant seals are called "cows," whereas males are called "bulls."

Page 33: False. Female ermines are much smaller and can be about half the size of male ermines.

Page 36: C. A baby seal is called a "pup."

Page 48: True. Leopard seals are the only seals that eat other warm-blooded animals, including other small seals.

Page 51: B. About 60 percent of the world's puffins are found in Iceland.

Page 53: A. A group of Arctic wolves is called a "pack."

Page 54: B. Alaskan Malamutes, Eskimo Dogs, and Samoyeds are considered sled dogs, along with others such as Siberian Huskies and Chinooks.

Page 59: False. Unlike most owls, snowy owls hunt during the day.

Page 63: D. All of the above! A walrus's tusks have many uses.